STRONG IS THE NEW PRETTY

A GUIDED JOURNAL
FOR GIRLS

KATE T. PARKER

WORKMAN PUBLISHING · NEW YORK

If you want to see the strongest person
I have ever met, turn to page 84.
This book is dedicated to her.

turn to page 84

⌒⌒ ♥ ⌒⌒

GRACE ADDISON BUNKE

(2003-2018),
your joy, courage, and heart inspire so many.
Knowing you and your story was a gift.

LIBRARY OF CONGRESS CATALOGING-IN-PUBLICATION DATA IS AVAILABLE.

ISBN 978-1-5235-0550-0

DESIGN BY SARA CORBETT

WORKMAN BOOKS ARE AVAILABLE AT SPECIAL DISCOUNTS WHEN PURCHASED
IN BULK FOR PREMIUMS AND SALES PROMOTIONS AS WELL AS FOR FUND-RAISING
OR EDUCATIONAL USE. SPECIAL EDITIONS OR BOOK EXCERPTS CAN ALSO BE CREATED
TO SPECIFICATION. FOR DETAILS, CONTACT THE SPECIAL SALES DIRECTOR AT
THE ADDRESS BELOW, OR SEND AN EMAIL TO SPECIALMARKETS@WORKMAN.COM.

WORKMAN PUBLISHING CO., INC.
225 VARICK STREET
NEW YORK, NY 10014-4381
WORKMAN.COM

WORKMAN IS A REGISTERED TRADEMARK
OF WORKMAN PUBLISHING CO., INC.

PRINTED IN CHINA
FIRST PRINTING SEPTEMBER 2018

10 9 8 7 6 5 4 3 2 1

INTRODUCTION

I wrote and photographed my first book,
Strong Is the New Pretty, to inspire young
girls to celebrate the strength in simply being
themselves. For this project, I knew I wanted
to make something that took the powerful
ideas and sentiments of the girls in that book
and put them into action. I created this journal
as a way to remind you of your own strength.
It's a place to write down your thoughts, your
ideas, your art, your words.

There are questions, activities, dares,
creative prompts, space for recording your
dreams and hopes and fears. I want you to get
out, explore, and think about the world around
you and your place in it. Fill these pages
with everything you discover, whenever and
however you like. Take your time and savor
every experience. And when you've had a bad
day or don't feel like yourself, come back to
these pages to show yourself just how strong
you truly are.

I'm so excited for you to start this journey.

Draw the first thing you see in the sky that is flying. A bug, plane, butterfly, kite, bird . . .

Draw a picture of yourself as a superhero. What does your cape look like? What is your superpower?

Use your voice! Think about something that you think is unfair or could be better in your school, town, city, state, or country. Write your notes here, and then send a letter to your school board, mayor, congressperson, senator, or the president to ask that it be changed.

MY NAME IS

I WOULD LIKE TO CHANGE

I DON'T LIKE IT BECAUSE

Write a song and sing it. It doesn't have to rhyme,
and you can sing it only for yourself.

Climb a tree. Make a paper airplane with a wish written inside, and send it flying.

Use this page to draft a thank-you letter to a coach, teacher, or other adult who inspires you. How do they inspire you? (And, if you're feeling brave, share it with the person.)

Make someone's day. Leave a nice note for someone who needs it, without the person knowing it's from you. Write your rough draft here.

Invent a new language. Write down some translations here.

strong

love

friend

hello

kind

girl

super

Save this page for when you're mad. Scribble here as hard as you need to.

Sometimes one page isn't enough.

Stand in front of a mirror, open your book wide to this page, and hold it in front of you facing the mirror. Say it out loud: I AM STRONG.

T2 MAI

Take a picture and paste it here.

WHAT ARE YOU MAKING?

HOW WILL YOU SELL IT?

HOW MUCH WILL IT COST?

What is the next difficult thing you have to do? How are you going to rise to the challenge? List three ways.

You are the host of your own TV show. You are an expert with a devoted fan base. What is your show about? What is the title? Draw it here.

"SHARE YOUR SHINE. OUR WORLD NEEDS MORE OF THAT." —CLEO WADE

What makes you beautiful?

....

....

....

....

....

....

....

....

....

....

Draw yourself in your dream job. What is it?
What do you look like? What are you doing?
What could you do today to get you there?

What are you good at? Like, *really* good at.

Draw a map to help you find your happy place. Where is it? Is it an actual place or is it doing something that makes you feel happy?

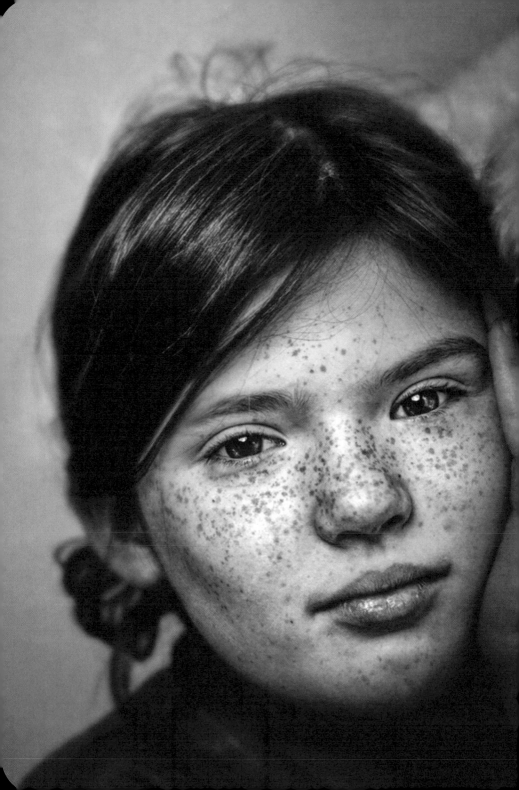

In what ways are you unique? List three things
about you that make you one-of-a-kind.

3

Write a mini play. Get some friends to perform it with you. Here are three potential titles to help you get started: *The Most Amazing Day Ever*, *The Magical Socks*, or *The Time I Was Elected President*.

What are the last three books you read?

1

2

3

Which was your favorite?

What were your favorite parts or characters?

How does an airplane fly? If you don't know, research it. Then describe it here in your own words.

Draw a picture of how you'd redo your bedroom to really make it yours. Include details that will make it feel like your most favorite place in the world.

Here is how to say "I am strong" in Spanish, Korean, Swahili, American Sign Language, and more. Learn these and then learn it in more languages!

Soy fuerte. (Soi FWEHR-teh.)	**SPANISH**
Я СИЛЬНА. (Ya syl'na.)	**UKRAINIAN**
나는 강하다. (Naneun ganghada.)	**KOREAN**
Ich bin stark. (Iç bin shtahk.)	**GERMAN**
Nina nguvu. (Neenah ng-GOO-voo.)	**SWAHILI**
Je suis forte. (Juh swee fort.)	**FRENCH**
Tokheča wamáš'ake. (Toe-kay-tchah wah-ma-shAH-ka.)	**LAKOTA**
私は強いです。(Watashi wa tsuyoidesu.)	**JAPANESE**
.أنا قوية (Ana ka-we-a.)	**ARABIC**

AMERICAN SIGN LANGUAGE

Make a piece of clothing out of a clean garbage bag. Sketch your design here. Use scissors and tape to assemble it. Put on your own garbage bag fashion show!

Think about what activity makes you happiest.
Draw a picture of yourself doing it.

What makes where you live special? Is it hot? Cold? Mostly flat? In the mountains? In a city? Draw a picture of your hometown here.

Six years from now, I will be . . .

Who is your hero? Write down a few reasons why. But more importantly, *tell them.*

(Here's a secret: You're someone's hero, too. Wouldn't *you* want to hear that?)

Trace your
hand here.
Decorate it
if you'd like!
Then give
yourself
a high five.

What was the best dream you ever
had? Draw a picture of it or write
about it here.

Do a good deed for someone. Surprise them with a note telling them how great they are, draw them a picture, and/or help them out in some way. Write about it here. (And good for you!)

Whom do you admire? Draw them here, and write your reasons why.

PERSON I ADMIRE

WHY I ADMIRE THEM

What scares you? List five things here.

1

2

3

4

5

How can you conquer one of the fears you wrote on the opposite page? What are three things you can do to make that fear not so big?

1

2

3

Use these two pages to draw your dream trip. Where are you going? With whom? What are you doing? Get specific!

When was the last time you laughed really hard?
What was it about? Write about it here.

Do something kind for someone you love, but this time, leave a note. On the bottom of this page, tell this person why you love them and why they deserved your kind act. Then tear it off and leave it where they'll find it.

TEAR/CUT HERE ✂

Eleven years from now, I will be . . .

Use this page to write down something new you'd like to learn (for example, a skill, a song, or a language). What are the steps you need to take to learn it?

TODAY'S DATE:

SOMETHING NEW:

NEXT STEPS:

Revisit this page in two weeks and write down your progress here.

TODAY'S DATE:

MY PROGRESS:

What does it feel like to be you? Draw a self-portrait. But don't draw yourself exactly as you look. Draw yourself as you *feel*. You can be any size, shape, or color—anything!

What is your biggest dream? Write it down in

BIG

letters. Then . . .

Write it in TINY letters down here. Snip or tear off the corner of this page and bury it in the ground. Decorate around the area where you buried it to remember the spot and what you wished for. Imagine it is a seed and help it grow.

TEAR/CUT HERE

Find a quiet place. Take ten deep breaths, counting to five on each inhale and exhale. Think about somewhere, someone, or something that makes you feel calm and happy.

Then draw your thoughts here.

Who is in your family? (P.S. They don't need to be related to you.) Draw them and write your favorite thing about each person underneath their picture.

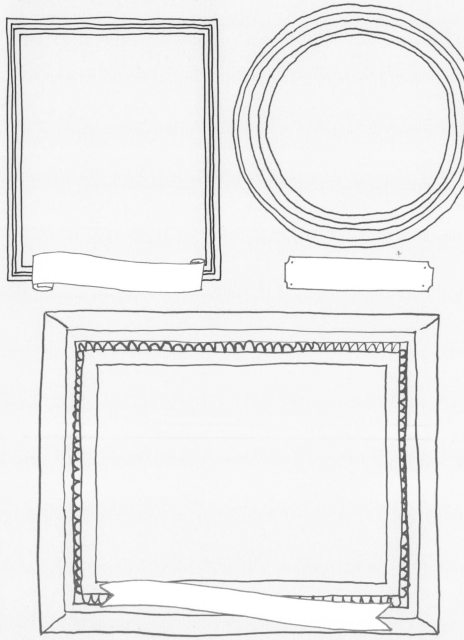

Go outside and explore! Find something green. Find something round. Find something yellow. Find something smooth. Find something rough. Find something multicolored. Trace or draw them here. Label and note where you found each one.

SOMETHING MULTICOLORED

SOMETHING ROUND

SOMETHING YELLOW

SOMETHING ROUGH

SOMETHING SMOOTH

SOMETHING GREEN

Decorate a rock. Use this page as your drop cloth—and don't be afraid to get messy. Make it stand out! Try stickers, paint, or markers. Make it beautiful in a way that inspires you.

Keep it as a good-luck charm to remind yourself of the beauty you created with your own hands.

STRONG IS THE NEW PRETTY

is the motto for this book. What is your motto? Write it here in bold letters:

Dress in a totally silly outfit and wear it out of the house—
to school, to the store, to the park. . . . Walk around like
everything is normal. Be aware of any stares or comments.
Draw a picture of yourself in your outfit here and write down
the funniest reactions you get.

MY NAME IS ....

I AM .... YEARS OLD.

MY BIRTHDAY IS .... AND
MY HALF BIRTHDAY IS ....

MY HERO IS ....

MY SUPERPOWER IS ....

I WISH I KNEW HOW TO ....

....

MY FAVORITE THING TO DO IS ....

....

MY FAVORITE SONG IS ....

....

I CANNOT LIVE WITHOUT ....

WHEN I AM SAD, ...
MAKES ME FEEL BETTER.

Create a treasure hunt for someone. Leave notes with clues that lead them to a gift you've made (a card, a paper flower, a decorated rock) as the prize. Jot your ideas here.

Check out the sky on a cloudy day. Look for shapes.
Look for a story. What do you see? Draw or write it here.

Where do you live? Find the farthest, most different place from where you are. What is it like there? What language do they speak? What is daily life like for girls your age there?

Twenty-two years from now, I will be . . .

On a rainy day, open your book to this this page, take it outside, and let a few drops fall on it. Try to catch one here! Once they dry, check out how the paper has changed.

Here are some fun things to do while out in the rain getting your page wet:

1 Make a mud pie.

2 Catch a raindrop in your mouth.

3 Jump in a puddle.

4 Find some worms.

5 Build a dam.

"BRAVE, STRONG WOMEN TALK TO PEOPLE INSTEAD OF ABOUT PEOPLE." —GLENNON DOYLE

Make a list of five things you can say when someone starts gossiping.

1

2

grit \'grit\ *noun*: courage and resolve; strength of character

What gives you grit?

What is your favorite food to eat?

**Ask someone to help you or teach yourself how
to prepare it. (Be safe!) Write the recipe here.**

Use this page to wipe your hands and rest your spoon when you're cooking.

What is something you really don't like doing,
but do it anyway because it's good for you?

Finish this phrase:

NEVER HAVE I EVER (BUT I REALLY WANT TO)

Draw a picture of it here.

If you could wave a magic wand and

SUPERSIZE

anything, what would it be? Why?

Design a T-shirt that you'd love
to see girls wearing everywhere.

Describe three of your friends. What do you love most about them? What is your favorite thing to do together? How are you alike? How are you different?

If you were in charge of your town/city, what changes would you make?

Go get muddy. Sign your name here with the mud.

Make a snack for someone you love. Pretend you're hosting a cooking show and your snack is getting judged on creativity, aroma, and taste. Have someone review your cooking here.

MY LEAST FAVORITE FOOD IS ....

....

THE SONG THAT GETS STUCK IN MY HEAD IS ....

....

....

I DON'T THINK ....

....

IS FAIR AND I AM GOING TO ....

....

....

....

....ABOUT IT.

SIGNED,...

....

What does the best day ever look like? Write a schedule of the day. Can you do at least one of these things today?

gender norms \ˈjen-dər ˈnȯrmz\ *plural noun*: a range of behaviors or attitudes that are generally considered acceptable, appropriate, or desirable for boys and girls

Next time you go to a toy store or clothing store, find three items in the girls' section that promote gender norms. Write or draw them here.

What are some stereotypes of girls? Can you think of three ways in which you meet those stereotypes and three ways you break them?

If you could go anywhere in the world, where would you go? Why? What and whom would you bring?

Think about a time when you failed at something (a test, an activity—anything). Did you keep going, and if so, how?

Trace one of your feet here.
(Or as much as you can fit!)

SKIN ON THE SOLES OF YOUR FEET IS THICKER THAN ANYWHERE ELSE ON YOUR BODY.

DID YOU KNOW THAT YOUR FOOT HAS 33 JOINTS, 26 BONES, 19 MUSCLES, AND 107 LIGAMENTS?

Where do your feet take you every day?

Grab a newspaper, book, or magazine in your house. Find three words you don't understand the meaning of, write them down, and go look them up. Add their definitions here.

Talk to the oldest female member of your family. Ask her to tell you a story about when she was your age. Write it down here.

If you could add one class to your school day,
what would it be, and why?

Find something that is broken in your house and take it apart (an old toy, for instance). Get some tools*—or whatever you need to see what's inside—and explore!

*Be safe and check with an adult first.

Draw a picture of someone in your family whom you love very much.

TEAR OR SNIP OFF THIS CORNER AND WRITE A LITTLE NOTE TO REMIND THE PERSON HOW MUCH YOU LOVE THEM.

Make up your own game. Use whatever is around you right now. The space you're in, the people (or lack of) that are there. Grab the first thing you see that can fit into your hand and make that the centerpiece of your new game. Write the rules here for how to play.

How are you strong? List three ways.

1

2

3

What do you wear or do because it's expected of you as a girl? Draw a few of those things here.

What do boys and men wear or do because it's expected of them? Do you wear or do any of those things? Draw a few of them here.

Draw what it feels like
to be sad, angry, happy,
and excited.

HAPPY

SAD

EXCITED

ANGRY

What can you learn today to be more self-sufficient?
It can be anything! Learn how to make your own lunch,
do your own laundry, clean your bathroom. Figure it out
and then stick with it so it can be part of your routine.

Can you wink? Can you roll your tongue? Curl your tongue?
Touch your tongue to your nose? Wiggle your ears? Raise
an eyebrow? Twitch your nose? Snap your fingers? What
quirky thing(s) can your amazing body do?

FLIP BOOK!

Draw a tiny picture and repeat it
in the same corner of the next 25
pages. Flip through the pages quickly
to see how your picture moves!

Fill in the blanks on this family tree with information about your family. Ask your parents, aunts, uncles, and grandparents to help you.

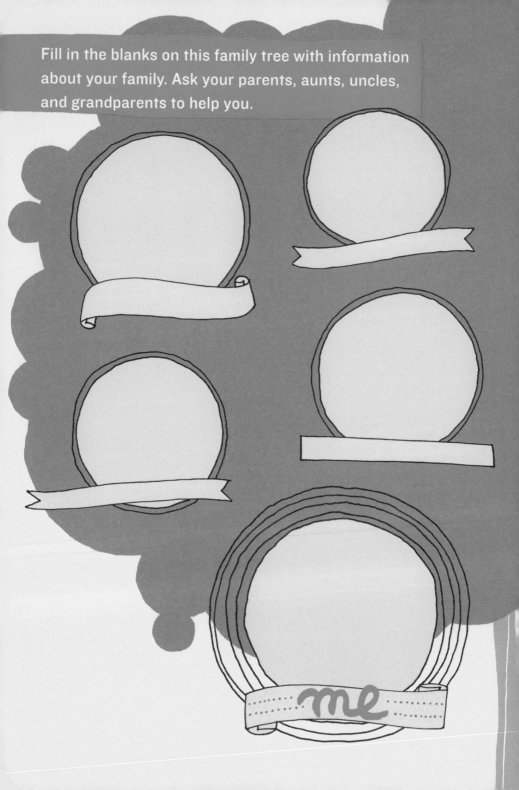

me

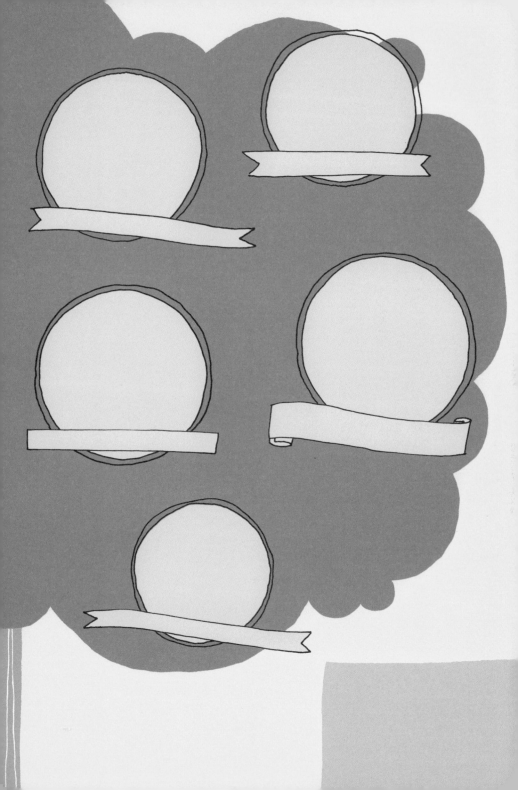

Place a picture of someone you admire in this frame. It can be a photo you paste or a drawing you make. Decorate the space around the picture with things they like and accomplishments they are proud of.

Think about someone who could use your help. Figure out how/when/why you will be helping them. Write a plan here and ask an adult if you need assistance executing your plan.

Play a game of Telephone starting with, "I am super strong and amazing."

What does the phrase turn into at the end? Write it here.

Create a course around your block, your yard, or even inside your home, and complete it. Can you navigate it faster next time? If your course is outdoors, change how you do it: walk, run, skip, scoot, skate, bike, or skateboard—whatever means you have to move, use it.

Draw yourself in your favorite place,
wearing your most comfortable clothes.

What was the hardest thing you've ever had to go through? How did you get through it? What did you learn?

Today at school, make your voice heard. Raise your hand, ask questions, or make suggestions. Write about what you did here.

Go somewhere you've never been and take notes. What does it look like? Smell like? Sound like? How is it different from other places you've been? (Or, go someplace familiar and challenge yourself to notice something you've never noticed before.)

EXPLORE!

MONDAY

Do something nice for someone who isn't always nice to you.

What did you do?

How did they react?

How did you feel after?

TUESDAY

Try a new physical activity like climbing a tree, running around, or doing fifty jumping jacks.

What did you do?

How did you feel immediately afterward?

How did you feel an hour later?

Weeklong Challenge

WEDNESDAY

Sit with someone new at lunch. (If you don't get to choose your seat, plan an after-school or weekend meet-up with someone new.)

Who did you sit with?

What questions did you ask to get to know

.... better?

What new things did you learn about

..................................?

How did you feel?

THURSDAY

Try a new food today! Something you've never, ever had before and maybe something that doesn't even sound very good. What was it? Write or draw about it here.

Rate it here: 1   2   3   4   5

YUCK!   YUM!

Describe it here:

FLAVOR

TEXTURE

AROMA

Smush a little bit of it right here:

FRIDAY

Figure out a new way to relax.
What makes you feel good
if you are stressed? (Taking
a bath? Reading a book?
Being outside?) Draw or
write your ideas here.

If you could make yourself invisible, where would you go? What would you do?

If you could go back in time to meet
anyone, who would it be, and why?

You have three wishes: two to help the world
and one just for you. What would you wish for?

You're a shape-shifter, which means you have the power to change your form or identity anywhere, at any time. What will you be?

If you could invent anything, what would you make? Draw a picture of how it works here.

Pick a word or phrase that lifts you up when you feel down. Write it here in the space provided and then decorate the whole page with that word or phrase. (For example, *brave* or *I've got this.*)

Dig through the recycling bin. Grab something that's still usable and repurpose it to make something new.

Draw a picture of how you'd redecorate any room in your home. Add furniture, pictures on the walls, paint colors, and anything else that would make it just right.

Take a "bath" in nature. Go outside with a blanket, find a spot in the sun or the shade, and sit quietly. Smell the smells, hear the sounds, see the sights, feel the air. Describe what you experience.

"THERE'S POWER IN LOOKING SILLY AND NOT CARING THAT YOU DO." —AMY POEHLER

Describe a time when you acted silly and didn't care. If you don't already have a story, make it your goal this week to get silly and then write about it here.

Interview someone you know who has a job that sounds interesting to you. Here are a few questions to help get you started.

1 What is your favorite thing about your job?

2 Describe a typical day.

3 What is the hardest part of your job?

4 What training or education do you have that led to this job?

5

6

7

8

Get moving for ten minutes. Cartwheel around the yard, skip around the house, jump up the steps, do push-ups, hold a plank for one minute. Try to make this a habit for a week. Use this page to write what you do and let your sweat drip here.

Imagine you are the tour guide for your town or neighborhood. What are the highlights—the best places to go and things to see and do—that you would share? Describe them here.

What is something that no one knows
about you? Do you wish people knew it?
Why or why not?

NAME:

AGE:

HOW YOU KNOW ME:

NAME:

AGE:

HOW YOU KNOW ME:

NAME:

AGE:

HOW YOU KNOW ME:

WHAT DO YOU ADMIRE ABOUT ME?

1

2

3

WHAT DO YOU ADMIRE ABOUT ME?

1

2

3

WHAT DO YOU ADMIRE ABOUT ME?

1

2

3

ACKNOWLEDGMENTS

Creating this journal was never even close to a solo job. I am very lucky and thankful to have amazing support all around me. First, a huge thank you to my family, Mike, E, Allie, and even Tobin (woof). You guys are my home and my heart. I love you. To my parents, thank you for putting up with us four kids and for still taking care of me at forty-one. The Stones and the Anthonys (even Dave), I appreciate you all and love you and your families so much.

Megan Nicolay, my editor—I always appreciate and admire your insight and care, and your ability to make everything I do way better than how it was when it started. I love working with you and am so thankful to have had the chance to do it twice now! Chloe Puton, Diana Griffin, Moira Kerrigan, Sara Corbett, Beth Levy, Rachael Mt. Pleasant, and the entire team at Workman, thank you for making beautiful books that matter. I'm really thankful to work with William Callahan, my agent—I appreciate your foresight, humor, and ability to keep me calm. And, Liz Dilworth, you're the best. I literally could not have done this without you and your organized mind.

Thank you to the Girl Scouts of the USA for generously allowing me to photograph some of your scouts and include them in these pages. Thank you, too, to Fernbank Museum of Natural History for your collaboration and kindness. And last, thank you to all the girls who allowed me to pick their brains in the writing of this journal—especially the third graders of Atlanta Academy and Girls on the Run of Decatur, Georgia.

ABOUT THE AUTHOR

KATE T. PARKER is a mother, wife, Ironman, and professional photographer who shoots both personal projects and commercial work for her clients. Her *Strong Is the New Pretty* photo series and bestselling book have led to collaborations with brands including Disney, Athleta, Kellogg's, and NBC. The project has also inspired Kate to launch a philanthropic arm of Strong Is the New Pretty, partnering with such organizations as Girls on the Run, Women's March, the Arthur M. Blank Family Foundation, GLAM4GOOD, and the BULLY Project, by investing in girls' health and education.

She lives with her family in Atlanta, Georgia. This is her second book.